# Patchwork
# Quilts

## Gloria McKinnon

# Contents

**Published by Creative House**
(an imprint of Sally Milner Publishing Pty Ltd)
PO Box 2104
Bowral NSW 2576
AUSTRALIA

© Gloria McKinnon

ISBN 1 877080 03 9

Printed in Hong Kong 1999
Reprinted in China 2002

*Editorial*
Managing Editor: Judy Poulos
Contributing Editor: Gloria McKinnon

*Photography*
Andrew Payne, Andrew Elton

*Styling*
Louise Owens, Kathy Tripp, Lisa Hilton,
Anne-Marie Unwin

*Illustrations*
Lesley Griffith

*Production and Design*
Production Editor: Anna Maguire
Design Manager: Drew Buckmaster
Production Coordinator: Meredith Johnston
Production Artists: Petra Rode, Lulu
Dougherty

# Patchwork Quilts

*Originally made from fabric scraps by frugal pioneer women, patchwork quilts have taken on wonderful decorative and creative aspects. This is not to say that all the early quilts were dull, practical pieces; on the contrary, many were quite beautiful in their simplicity. Those that remain in museums and private collections tell us a great deal about the lives and aspirations of their makers.*

*The patchwork quilts in this book follow on those early traditions, but take advantage of the advent of the sewing machine and new quick-cutting and quick-piecing techniques.*

*Much of the pleasure of making quilts comes from the selection of the fabrics to make each one. Quilters call this 'playing' with the fabric. If you like one of the designs given in this book, but not the colour scheme or the choice of fabric, don't be limited by what you see. Be creative and give your quilt it's uniqueness by choosing fabrics and colours that reflect your personal taste.*

# Colourwash Quilt Wallhanging

STITCHED BY YAN PRING

*Fabric-aholics! Here is your chance to use up your favourite pieces and be a watercolour artist at the same time.*

Colourwash quilts were pioneered by Deidre Amsden of London, England. The focus here is on the colour effects that emerge from the light values of the fabrics, from very, very light to very, very dark. Choose multicoloured large- and small-scale prints with various values, and look for fabrics with special appeal, either in colour or theme.

**Finished size:** 98 cm x 133 cm ($38^1/_2$ in x $52^1/_2$ in)

## Materials

- 6 cm ($2^1/_4$ in) squares of fabric in the following numbers and values: seventy-nine very light, fifty medium light, forty-nine large-scale prints, twenty-one medium dark, forty-one very dark
- 10 cm (4 in) of plain fabric for the first border
- 15 cm (6 in) of print fabric for the second border
- 40 cm (15 in) each of a small floral print and a large floral print for the wide border
- 40 cm (15 in) of fabric for the binding
- 130 cm (51 in) of fabric for the backing
- 97 cm x 130 cm (38 in x 51 in) of wadding
- quilting thread
- machine-sewing thread

## Method

1 Following the quilt diagram, stitch groups of sixteen squares together to form blocks. Chain-piecing will speed things up (Figs 1, 2 and 3).

2 Stitch the blocks together in the order indicated in figure 4 to form the colourwash centre of the quilt.

### For the borders

1 Cut 3 cm ($1^1/_4$ in) wide strips from the plain fabric for the first border. Sew them to the short sides first, then to the top and bottom.

2 Cut 4.5 cm ($1^3/_4$ in) wide strips from the fabric for the second border. Attach them in the same way as the first border.

3 Cut 20 cm (8 in) wide strips from the fabrics for the wide border. Attach the small floral print border to the left-hand side first, then to the top. Attach the large floral print border to the right-hand side first, then to the bottom (Fig. 5).

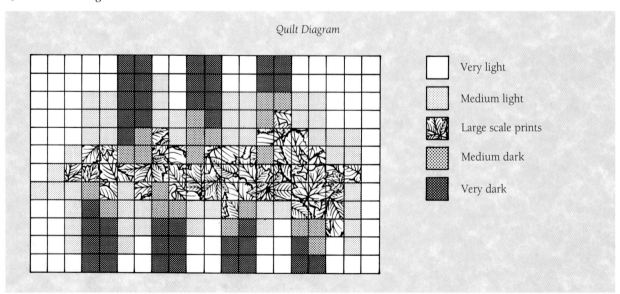

*Quilt Diagram*

☐ Very light

▦ Medium light

❧ Large scale prints

▨ Medium dark

▓ Very dark

## Quilting

**1** Lay the backing fabric, face down, on a suitable surface and tape it down so it does not move. Place the wadding on top and the completed quilt top on top of that, face upwards. Baste from the centre out to the edges and around the edges.

**2** Quilt all over the top in swirling lines, following the floral patterns. Trim the backing and the wadding to the size of the top.

## Finishing

Cut the binding fabric into 7 cm (3 in) wide strips. Join them together to make one long strip. Fold the strip over double with the wrong sides together and the raw edges even. Pin the binding around the right side of the quilt with the raw edges even. Stitch with a 6 mm ($^1/_4$ in) seam. Turn the binding over onto the back of the quilt and stitch it in place, either by hand or by machine.

Don't forget to sign and date your quilt.

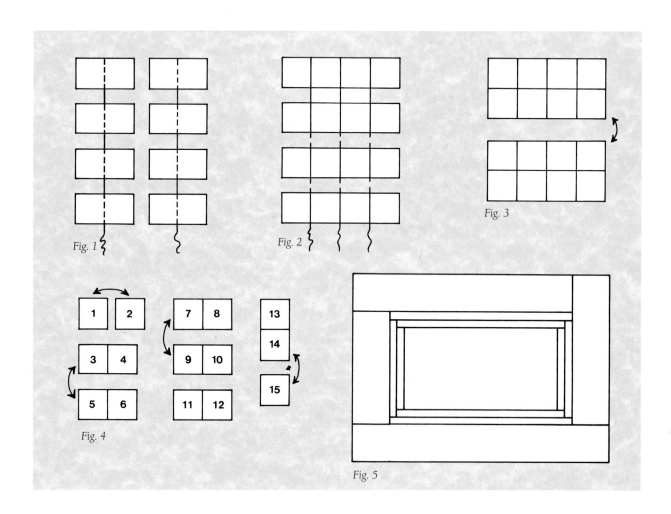

Fig. 1

Fig. 2

Fig. 3

Fig. 4

Fig. 5

# Fan Quilt

### MADE BY ANNE'S GLORY BOX

*This elegant Liberty quilt would complement any decor. Buttons, ribbons and charms are the wonderful personal touches that will make this quilt your own.*

**Finished size:** 120 cm x 160 cm (47$\frac{1}{2}$ in x 63 in)

## Materials

- ✿ 1.5 m (1$\frac{3}{4}$ yd) of homespun for the background
- ✿ 20 cm (8 in) of each of eight Liberty cotton prints
- ✿ 4 m (4$\frac{1}{2}$ yd) of 12 mm ($\frac{1}{2}$ in) wide insertion lace edging
- ✿ 1.4 m (1$\frac{1}{2}$ yd) of plain fabric for the borders
- ✿ 1.4 m (1$\frac{1}{2}$ yd) of Liberty fabric for the first large border
- ✿ 2.4 m (2$\frac{2}{3}$ yd) of Liberty's 'Strawberry Thief' for the outer border and binding
- ✿ 3.3 m (3$\frac{2}{3}$ yd) of Liberty print for the backing
- ✿ 130 cm (51 in) of wadding
- ✿ assorted silk ribbons, buttons, trinkets and charms
- ✿ matching sewing thread and hand-sewing needles
- ✿ cardboard for the templates
- ✿ template plastic
- ✿ fineline permanent marker pen
- ✿ sharp pencil

## Method

See the Templates and the Quilting Design on page 10. The templates do not include seam allowances. 6 mm ($\frac{1}{4}$ in) seam allowances should be added when you are cutting out.

**Note:** The fans are assembled and appliquéd by hand. The quilt top is then assembled by machine and machine-quilted.

### For the fans

1 Trace the templates onto the template plastic with the marker pen. Using this template and remembering to add seam allowances, cut out eight fan shapes from each of seven Liberty prints. Cut out fifty-six cardboard templates without seam allowances.

2 Baste the fabric over the cardboard template on the two long sides and the top, ensuring that all the edges are smooth.

3 Arrange the seven elements of the fan, then sew them together by placing two elements with the right sides facing and overstitching along the long edge. Do not stitch through the cardboard. When all seven elements are joined, press carefully on the wrong side with a hot iron to establish the crease at the top edge. Carefully remove the cardboard.

4 Cut eight 21.5 cm (8$\frac{1}{2}$ in) squares of homespun for the background. Mark the 6 mm ($\frac{1}{4}$ in) seam allowance around the outside of the square. Baste the two outside edges of the fan to the background square so that the ends of the curved edge lie 2.5 cm (1 in) from the seam allowance (Fig. 1).

5 Open out the seam allowance on the two outside elements of the fan and lay the pressed fold mark along the seam allowance line of the square.

6 Cut eight 50 cm (20 in) long pieces of the insertion lace. Gather the lace gently and evenly to fit the top edge of the fan. Tuck the edge of the lace just under the edge of the fan. Appliqué the top edge of the fan into position, stitching through the lace.

### For the fan centres

1 Make a plastic template of the centre of the fan and cut eight cardboard templates the same. Using the plastic template, cut eight centres from the last of the Liberty fabrics, remembering to add seam allowances.

2 Baste the fabric over the cardboard templates along the top edge only. To ensure a smooth edge, smooth the fabric with your thumb and bring it into small pleats at the back. Do not stitch over the seam allowances on the straight edges. It is also a good idea to put a couple of stitches through the centre of the cardboard and fabric to hold them securely. Press well, then remove the cardboard.

3 Appliqué the fan centres over the ends of the fans. Baste the free edges to the background fabric to hold it in position.

## Assembling

**Note:** Cut all the border strips down the length of the fabric.

**1** From the plain fabric for the borders, cut four 10 cm (4 in) wide strips and set them aside. From the same fabric, cut the following:

**A** twelve strips 5.5 cm x 21.5 cm ($2^{1}/_{4}$ in x $8^{1}/_{2}$ in);

**B** two strips 5.5 cm x 33 cm  ($2^{1}/_{4}$ in x 13 in);

**C** two strips 5.5 cm x 87.5 cm ($2^{1}/_{4}$ in x $34^{1}/_{2}$ in);

**D** one strip 5.5 cm x 93.5 cm ($2^{1}/_{4}$ in x $36^{3}/_{4}$ in).

**2** Attach two **A** strips to two fan blocks (Fig. 2) and make two rows of three fan blocks with four **A** strips (Fig. 3).

**3** From the background fabric cut three 26.5 cm ($10^{1}/_{2}$ in) squares. Cut each one in half diagonally to produce six **E** triangles for the sides of the quilt. Cut another 27.5 cm ($10^{3}/_{4}$ in) square. Cut it into four diagonally to produce four **F** triangles for the corners of the quilt.

**4** Join the quilt top, following the piecing diagram in figure 4. Trim the edges of the quilt to 6 mm ($^{1}/_{4}$ in) seam.

### For the borders

**1** For the first Liberty border, cut four 5 cm (2 in) wide strips down the length of the fabric. The plain border strips are already cut. For the outer Liberty border, we have used a 'one-way' fabric which needed to be pieced to achieve the length required. Cut three 15 cm (6 in) wide strips across the width of the fabric and join them end to end. This will do the shorter sides. Cut two 15 cm (6 in) wide strips down the length of the fabric for the other sides.

**2** Matching the centres of each of the three borders, join them together in the correct order in 6 mm ($^{1}/_{4}$ in) seams. Press the seams towards the outer border.

**3** Find and mark the centre of each side of the quilt top. Matching the centres, attach the joined borders to the quilt top. Note that there is an overlap at each end.

**4** Lay the quilt top on a flat surface so the borders are lying flat and square. To make the mitred corner, fold the top layer of border so that the seams match perfectly with the borders underneath (Fig. 5). Press the fold carefully, then stitch along the fold for the perfect mitre. Trim the overhang.

## Quilting

**1** Make a template of the quilting design. Using the pencil, transfer the quilting design to the side triangles on the quilt top.

**2** Cut and rejoin the backing fabric so that it is the correct size. Lay the backing fabric face down on a table or on the floor. Place the wadding on top and the quilt top on top of that, face upwards. Smooth out all the wrinkles as you place each layer. Secure the layers with basting, beginning at the centre and radiating out to the corners and sides. If you are planning to machine-quilt, you can use safety pins instead of basting, removing the safety pins as you quilt. The fans and borders on this quilt have been machine-quilted and the side triangles have been hand-quilted.

## Finishing

**1** Trim the backing and the wadding so they are even with the quilt top.

**2** Cut four 5.5 cm ($2^{1}/_{4}$ in) wide strips for the binding. Fold the strips over double with the wrong sides together. Sew the binding to the right side of the quilt with the raw edges even. Sew the binding to the sides first, then fold the binding over to the back of the quilt. Sew the binding to the top and bottom of the quilt, then fold the binding over to the back of the quilt. Slipstitch all the binding in place.

**3** Sew on all the embellishments (charms, silk ribbon bows, buttons etc) you would like to include.

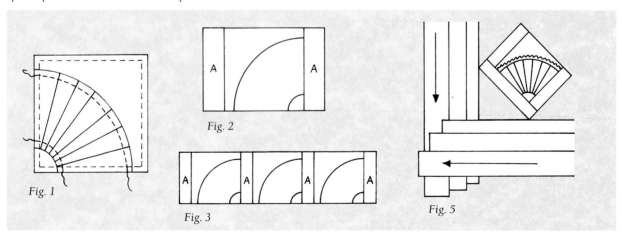

Fig. 1

Fig. 2

Fig. 3

Fig. 5

*Fig. 4*

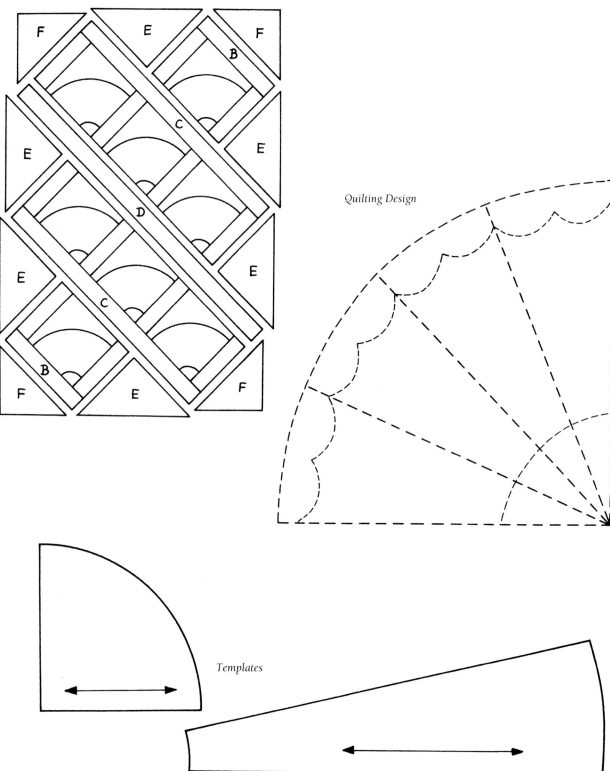

Quilting Design

Templates

# Log Cabin Quilt

MADE BY FAY KING

*The Log Cabin quilt has been a favourite over many years, and was often made from small fabric scraps left from dressmaking and from clothing remnants. This quilt has a real scrap-bag look and is made from many, many different fabrics.*

Organise your fabrics into lights and darks, using a colour theme. The lights in this quilt are warm and the darks use a lot of reds and navies. Beyond this, there is no planning of colour. When the fabrics are cut into strips, they are placed into a light pile and a dark pile. The choice of strips for the quilt is random.

This quilt is made stitching strips onto a premarked foundation fabric.

Total number of blocks: 60

**Finished size:** approximately 128.75 cm x 202.5 cm (51½ in x 81 in)

## Materials

- ❧ 2.6 m (2¾ yd) of a cream or white evenweave fabric, such as fine lawn, for the foundation
- ❧ light and dark fabrics cut into 4 cm (1½ in) strips. (If you are buying fabrics, buy 20 cm (8 in) of a number of fabrics)
- ❧ sixty 5 cm (2 in) squares in dark colours for the block centres
- ❧ 2 m (2¼ yd) of fabric for the borders
- ❧ 2.8 m (3¼ yd) of fabric for the backing
- ❧ 2.2 m (2⅓ yd) of wadding
- ❧ Pigma pen
- ❧ five hanks of stranded cotton to tie the quilt
- ❧ straw needles

## Method

See the Block Foundation Pattern on the Pull Out Pattern Sheet.

### Cutting

From the foundation fabric, cut sixty 21.5 cm (8½ in) squares. Onto these squares, trace the whole log cabin block using the Pigma pen. These lines are your stitching lines.

The marked side of the block will be called the wrong side and the unmarked side will be called the right side. Strips should be attached on the right side around the centre square in an anticlockwise direction.

### For the block

1 Pin or baste a 5 cm (2 in) square on the centre of the right side of the foundation fabric with the face up.

2 Lay a light strip face down over the centre. Turn the whole piece to the wrong side and stitch the first line, locking the thread at each end. Turn back to the right side, fold the strip into position and press.

3 The second strip is also light. Lay it face down on the right side in its position. Stitch on the wrong side. Fold the strip back and press as before. Trim the strip to fit.

4 The next two strips are dark. When they are attached as the first two, you will have completed one round. Each new round starts with a light fabric and on the same side as step 1. There are four rounds to complete the block. Make sixty blocks in this way.

## Assembling

If the fabrics are randomly selected, there is no need to lay out the blocks in any order. Use the placement diagram below to join the blocks into the quilt top.

Join the blocks by stitching on the outside line of the block, pinning carefully to ensure matching seams. Make ten rows of six blocks each, then join the rows into two sets of five rows. Finally, join the two halves through the centre. When joining the rows, press the seams in alternate directions so that they snuggle together.

### *For the borders*

Cut four long strips, each 10 cm (4 in) wide. Attach the strips to the long sides first, using 6 mm (¹/₄ in) seams, then attach the borders to the top and bottom of the quilt top.

## Tying

1 Cut and rejoin the backing fabric to fit the quilt top. The join will run across the quilt.

2 Lay the backing fabric face down on a hard surface with the wadding on top, then the quilt top on top of that, face upwards.

3 Baste from the centre to the edges so that the layers are securely held, then baste around the outside edge.

4 Tie the quilt at regular intervals, starting from the centre and working to the edges. Each block should be tied as shown in figure 1. Using the full six strands of the stranded cotton, stitch from the front to the back and to the front again, coming up about 3 mm (¹/₈ in) away. Repeat this step. Tie the two ends in a reef knot (right over left, then left over right). Trim the ends to approximately 1 cm (³/₈ in).

## Finishing

To finish the edges, turn under a 6 mm (¹/₄ in) seam allowance on the border fabric. Trim the wadding to the size of the quilt top. Trim the backing fabric 2.5 cm (1 in) larger. Fold the backing over the wadding (between the wadding and the top) and slipstitch the edges of the top and backing together.

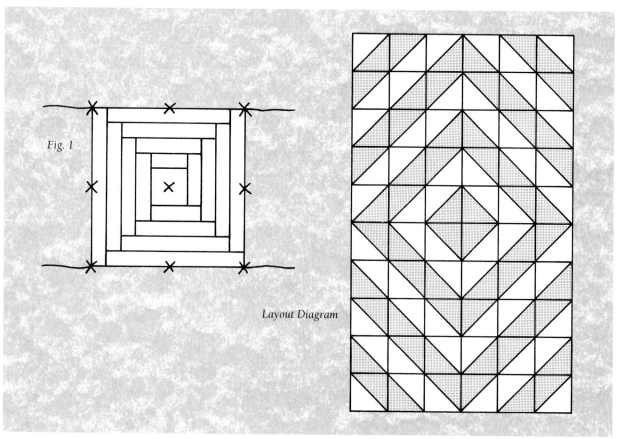

*Fig. 1*

*Layout Diagram*

# Country Barns Wallhanging

MADE BY FAY KING

*This small hand-pieced quilted wallhanging is a great way to use a lot of country-style fabrics from your scrap bag.*

**Finished size:** 96 cm x 105 cm (38 in x 41 in)

## Materials

- small pieces of floral, checked and striped fabric for the barns (you can make each barn the same or each one quite different)
- Piecemakers crewel needles, size 9
- cotton threads to match the fabrics
- 1 m (1 1/8 yd) of fabric for the backing
- 100 cm x 109 cm (39 in x 43 in) of wadding
- 25 cm (10 in) of navy fabric for the first border
- 35 cm (14 in) of fabric for the second border
- cardboard for the templates
- H or HB propelling pencil
- ruler

## Method

See the Templates on the Pull Out Pattern Sheet.

### Preparation

Trace the templates from the pattern sheet. Transfer each one to the cardboard and carefully cut it out. Make nine cardboard templates for each shape.

### For each barn

1 Place each cardboard template onto the back of a fabric piece and draw around it. Cut out the piece, adding a 6 mm (1/4 in) seam allowance. Take special care when cutting out the barn roof as it will only fit if cut one way.

2 Baste the fabric over the cardboard, making sure that it sits square and straight.

**Hint:** When basting the fabric over the cardboard, centre the cardboard on the wrong side of the fabric, then fold and stitch until it is quite secure, placing a stitch to hold any fabric folds. For triangles, do not try to fold in all the fabric at the corners. Simply fold over the seam allowance and baste it in place, leaving a flap of fabric at the corner. This will give you nice sharp points with not too much bulk.

3 When all the cardboard pieces for one block have been covered, lay the block out, ready for assembly. Place the first two pieces to be joined with the right sides together. Begin stitching approximately 6 mm (1/4 in) from the left-hand corner, stitch up to that corner, then down to the right-hand corner. Topstitch back along the seam for approximately 6 mm (1/4 in) to secure. Snip the thread, leaving a tail approximately 6 mm (1/4 in) long. When you are stitching, catch only the fabric, not the cardboard. Join all the other pieces for the block in this way. Make nine blocks.

## Assembling

1 Cut six pieces of cardboard for the sashing, each 5 cm x 25 cm (2 in x 10 in). Cut the fabric and cover the cardboard in the same way as for the barns.

2 Join three blocks together in a row with a length of sashing in between.

3 Join three rows together to form the centre of the quilt, taking care that all the corners meet accurately.

### For the first border

1 Measure the width and length of the quilt. Cut cardboard strips 4 cm (1 1/2 in) wide and these lengths. Cut the navy fabric and cover the cardboard strips as before.

2 Cut 4 cm (1 1/2 in) squares from the cardboard for the corners. Cut out the fabric and cover the cardboard squares as before.

3 Attach one square to each end of the top and bottom borders, then attach the side borders.

### For the outer border

1 Measure the quilt carefully, then cut cardboard and fabric to these measurements as before.

2 Attach the side borders to the quilt, then the top and bottom borders.

### Finishing

1 Carefully remove all the cardboard pieces by undoing or snipping all the basting threads. Press the quilt top well.

2 Baste under the seam allowances around the edges of the quilt.

3 Lay the backing face down on a table with the wadding on top and the quilt top on top of that, face upwards. Baste the layers together securely.

4 Quilt around the pieces as indicated in the quilting diagram below or in a design of your own.

5 Trim the backing to 2.5 cm (1 in) bigger than the quilt top all around. Trim the wadding to the exact size of the quilt top. Fold the excess backing over the wadding, under the edge of the quilt top. Slipstitch the edges together.

6 Make a sleeve for the back of the wallhanging so you can hang it up.

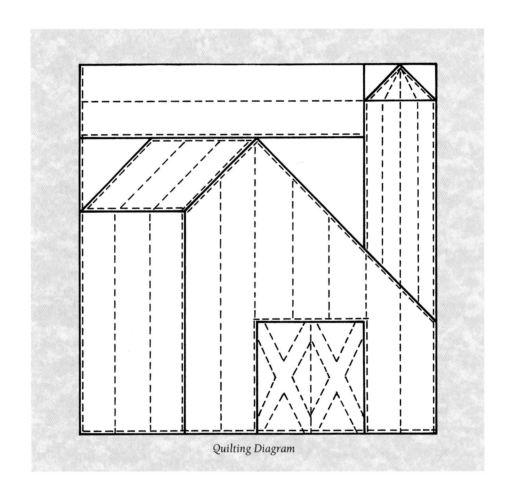

*Quilting Diagram*

# Blossom Basket Quilt

## Made by Yan Pring

*Compose a symphony of springtime with a charming Victorian basket to hold a bouquet of colourwash blooms.*

**Finished size:** 117 cm x 122 cm (46 in x 48 in)

## Materials

- scraps of fabrics including large florals, medium florals, small florals, small leaves and sprigs, large leaves, fabrics for the basket, medium light and very light fabrics for the background, and medium blue fabrics
- 1.6 m (1³/₄ yd) of lace edging (Yan has used several different laces)
- 76 cm (30 in) of 1.2 cm (¹/₂ in) wide velvet ribbon for the bow
- 90 cm (36 in) of cotton bias binding for the handle
- strips of various widths of fabric for the inner borders
- 45 cm (18 in) of 140 cm (55 in) wide furnishing cotton for the outer border
- Perle Cotton to match the velvet ribbon
- 1.6 m (1³/₄ yd) of low-loft wadding
- 122 cm x 127 cm (48 in x 50 in) of fabric for the backing
- 30 cm (12 in) of fabric for the binding

## Method

See the Placement Diagram on page 20.

### For the colourwash centre

1 Cut a generous selection of fabrics in each category into 5 cm (2 in) squares. Make sure you include yellows, blues and lilacs for a spring bouquet.

2 To make the half-square triangles on the sides of the basket, place a 'basket' square on top of a medium light background square, with the right sides together. Stitch across the diagonal, trim off half of the basket square and flip the other over. Take care to trim the correct half or you will need to begin again (Fig. 1). Press well.

3 Arrange the squares to give a pleasing harmony of colour, following the placement diagram on page 20. Note there are eighteen squares across and twenty squares down. Sew the squares together to form the colourwash centre of the quilt.

### For the handle

1 To make the handle, hand-sew the inner edge of the bias binding in place, using a blind hemstitch. Pin the edge of the lace underneath the other side of the handle, then stitch it down, neatening the ends.

2 Tie the velvet ribbon into a bow and attach it to the handle with French knots using the Perle Cotton.

3 Trim the basket with lace as shown.

### For the borders

This quilt has been designed so that the basket sits within a lovely frame. Of course, you can design your own borders. To re-create the design shown here, cut your fabrics to the measurements shown on the border diagram on page 20, where each square represents 3.5 cm (1¹/₂ in). Remember to add 1 cm (³/₈ in) for each seam allowance.

### Quilting

1 Place the backing face down on a table with the wadding on top and the quilt top on top of that, face upwards. Baste the three layers together securely.

2 Quilt the wallhanging in any pattern you prefer. Yan has quilted only around the borders of her quilt.

### Finishing

1 Cut the binding fabric into 5 cm (2 in) wide strips. Join strips together to achieve the required length.

2 Fold the binding over double with the right sides together. Stitch the binding to the top and bottom of the quilt with the raw edges even. Turn the binding to the back of the quilt and slipstitch it in place. Repeat for the sides of the quilt.

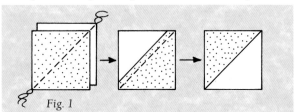

*Fig. 1*

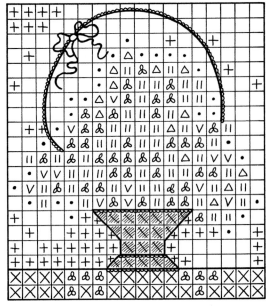

Placement Diagram

| | | |
|---|---|---|
| ⚘ | | Large florals |
| ‖ | | Medium florals |
| △ | | Small florals |
| • | | Small leaves and sprigs |
| V | | Large leaves |
| ▨ | | Basket fabrics |
| ✚ | | Medium light fabrics |
| ☐ | | Very light fabrics |
| ✕ | | Medium blue fabrics |

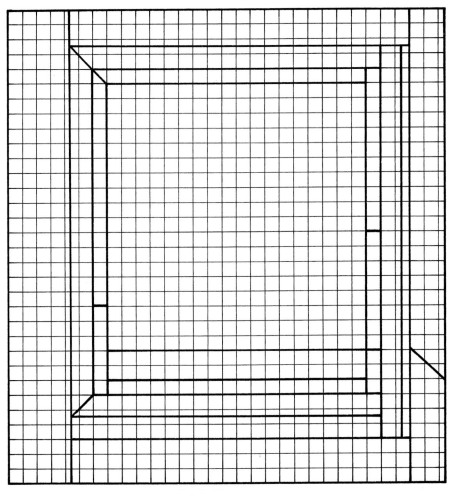

Border Diagram

☐ = 3·5 x 3·5 cm (1½ x 1½ in)

# Drunkard's Path Quilt

MADE BY DIANA MARKS, CALIFORNIA

*This quilt is a great way to use up your scraps or charm pieces you have been collecting.*

Diana had been collecting off-white fabrics when she won the fat quarter lottery in the craft forum on Compuserve. These 'on-line' quilters come from all over the world, including Australia.

There are many different ways of constructing Drunkard's Path. Some methods require pins, some clipping, some use freezer paper. We have found Anita Murphy's pinless technique to be the easiest and fastest.

We wish to thank Chitra Publications, publishers of *Traditional Quiltworks* for allowing us to reproduce the quilt, made by Lynn Mann.

**Finished size:** 137 cm x 165 cm (54 in x 66 in)

## Materials

- 3.6 m (4 yd) total of different lights/neutrals
- 1.83 m (2 yd) total of different darks
- 1.14 m (1¼ yd) of dark fabric for the border and binding
- 3.6 m (4 yd) of fabric for the backing
- 147 cm x 175 cm (58 in x 60 in) of wadding
- 15 cm (6 in) bias square
- small rotary cutter
- small and large self-healing cutting mats

## Method

See the Templates on the Pull Out Pattern Sheet.

### Cutting

**Note:** The templates are full size and include the 6 mm (¼ in) seam allowance. Use the small rotary cutter to cut around the template keeping the rotary cutter straight. If you cut on the small mat it will be easier to turn as you are cutting.

**1** Cut one 11.5 cm (4½ in) strip from each of your scraps. If you are using charm pieces, 12.7 cm (5 in) or 15 cm (6 in) pieces will be fine. Do not cut these into strips. You may also need some 14 cm (5½ in) strips from your lights for the border, so don't cut everything.

**2** Cut the following pieces:
48 A from the light scraps;

240 A from the medium or dark scraps;

48 B from the medium or dark scraps;

240 B from the light scraps; and

If you have cut 14 cm (5 ½ in) light strips for the border, cut them into 14 cm (5 ½ in) squares, then cut them along both diagonals. Alternatively, using template C, cut 96 triangles from light scraps. Piece these to make twenty-four 14 cm (5½ in) squares.

**3** Cut three 4 cm x 114 cm (1⅝ in x 44 in) dark solid strips and nine 5 cm x 114 cm (2 in x 44 in) dark solid strips for the borders.

**4** Cut six 7.5 cm x 114 cm (3 in x 44 in) dark solid strips for the binding.

### Piecing

**1** Place an L-shaped piece on top of a pie-shaped piece, with the right sides together (Fig. 1). Take no more than three or four stitches, very slowly. Leaving your needle in the fabric, bring the L-shaped piece back over the pie-shaped piece with the raw edges matching (Fig. 2). Continue in this way, making sure you have an accurate 6 mm (¼ in) seam allowance. Do not be alarmed if the bottom edges do not match up perfectly. Press the seam allowance towards the pie-shaped piece. You can use your bias square to even out your pieces to 9 cm (3½ in) squares before joining them into rows. As you become more comfortable with the technique, you can begin chain-piecing.

**2** Take four Drunkard's Path squares with light As and twelve with dark As (Figs 3 and 4). Arrange them as shown, with the light As in the corners (Fig. 5). Stitch the squares into rows, then stitch the rows together to complete one block.

**3** Lay the blocks out in four rows of three blocks each. Sew the blocks together into rows, then sew the rows together to complete the quilt top.

## For the borders

**1** Centre and stitch a 2.5 cm x 114 cm (1 in x 44 in) dark solid strip to the top and bottom of the quilt.

**2** Take the three 4 cm x 114 cm (1⅝ in x 44 in) dark solid strips. Cut one in half and sew the two halves to the other two pieces. Then centre and sew these strips to the left and right sides of the quilt.

**3** Take fifteen Drunkard's Path squares and fifteen of the light scrap triangles. Arrange them as shown in figure 6. You can stitch the squares and triangles together by working in diagonal rows. Make a second border like the first one.

**4** Sew the border units to the top and bottom edges of the quilt, positioning each border unit with its longer side touching the dark solid border.

**5** Take twenty-one Drunkard's Path squares and twenty-one light scrap triangles. Arrange them in a border unit similar to the ones you've already stitched, but instead of having nine triangles along the longer side, there will be twelve. Make a second border unit the same.

**6** Sew the border units to the left and right sides of the quilt. Again, position them so that their longer side is against the dark solid border.

**7** Arrange six Drunkard's Path squares and six light scrap triangles as shown in figure 7. Stitch them together, making a corner unit for the border. Make four corner units in the same way. Join one to each corner of the quilt.

**8** Take four of the 5 cm (2 in) wide dark solid strips and sew them together in pairs. Centre and sew these to the left and right sides of the quilt.

**9** Take four more of the 5 cm (2 in) wide strips and sew them in pairs. Cut the remaining 5 cm (2 in) wide strip in half and sew half to each pair.

## Quilting

**1** Press the quilt top well. Assemble the quilt sandwich, then baste through all thicknesses with lines of stitching approximately 10 cm (4 in) apart.

**2** Quilt in a design of your choice – this quilt requires little more than outline quilting.

## Binding

Fold the binding strips over double with the wrong sides together. Stitch the binding to the right side of the sides of the quilt with the raw edges matching. Turn the binding to the back of the quilt and slipstitch it into place. Bind the top and the bottom in the same way.

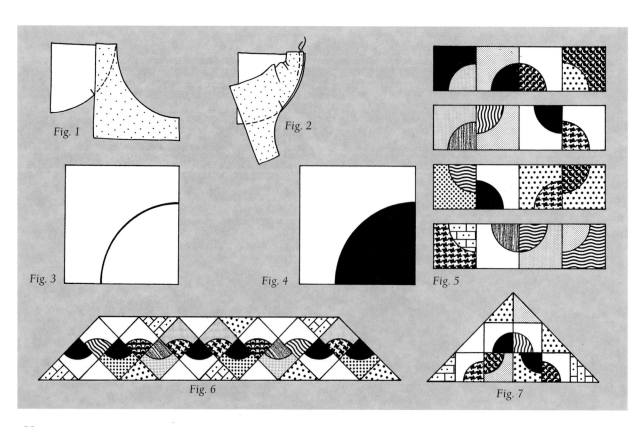

Fig. 1  Fig. 2  Fig. 3  Fig. 4  Fig. 5  Fig. 6  Fig. 7

# The Sisters

## MADE BY PAT PALMER, CALIFORNIA

*These saucy sisters will add cheer to any wall in your home.*

**Finished size:** 102 cm x 104 cm (40 in x 41 in)

## Materials

- ✄ fabric for the dolls, clothes, wings, boots, hair
- ✄ two fabrics for the borders
- ✄ 112 cm (44 in) square of fabric for the backing
- ✄ 80 cm (32 in) of fabric for the background
- ✄ 112 cm (44 in) square of Pellon or Rayfelt
- ✄ scraps of lace
- ✄ fourteen small buttons
- ✄ two buttons or beads
- ✄ pinking shears
- ✄ Pigma pens or fabric marker pens
- ✄ dark quilting thread, Burgundy or Navy
- ✄ hank of Perle Cotton
- ✄ template plastic
- ✄ small piece of cardboard
- ✄ black fineline permanent marker pen
- ✄ piece of old sock or sweater
- ✄ polyester fibre fill

## Method

See the Templates on the Pull Out Pattern Sheet.

## Preparation

Trace the templates and cut them out of the template plastic. Add 6 mm (1/4 in) seam allowances all around when cutting the pieces from the fabric.

### For the background

1 Cut the following: a piece 74 cm x 76 cm (29 in x 30 in) from the background fabric; four 5 cm (2 in) wide strips from the first border fabric; four 11 cm (4 1/4 in) wide strips from the second border fabric.

2 Measure in 19 cm (7 1/2 in) from both sides of the background piece. Press along these lines to mark the placement for the dolls.

3 Measure 11.5 cm (4 1/2 in) from the top of the background piece. Press along this line to mark the placement of the dolls' heads.

### For the arms and legs

1 Cut out four leg, four arm, four boot and four hand pieces for each doll. Sew the boots to the legs and the hands to the arms. Press the seam allowances open.

2 Using a small machine stitch and with the right sides together, join the pieces together in pairs, leaving the top edges open. Clip carefully into the curves and turn the pieces through to the right side.

3 Fill the hands/arms softly with the fibre fill up to the last 1 cm (3/8 in). Stitch the fingers either by hand or by machine. Fill the legs softly one-third of the way up the leg. Tie a knot for the knee, then continue to fill up to 1 cm (3/8 in) from the top.

### For the wings

Cut eight wing shapes roughly from fabric and four from Pellon or Rayfelt. Place the wing shapes together in pairs with the Pellon or Rayfelt in between. Quilt the outline of the wings, using the dark thread, then cut out the wings to the actual shape, using the pinking shears. Baste the wings into position on the background fabric.

### For the head

Cut out the fabric for the head, then trace the face outline onto the fabric, using the Pigma pens or the marker pens. Baste the fabric over a cardboard template, then press it well to ensure the curves are smooth. Remove the template and appliqué the head into position.

### For the body

1 Pin the arms and legs into position with the seams to the centre front and back.

2 Baste, then appliqué the body into position over the arms and legs making sure that the stitching is secure and goes

right through all thicknesses of fabric, especially over the arms and legs.

## For the skirt

1 Cut a 24 cm x 28 cm (9½ in x 11 in) fabric piece for the skirt. Stitch a small hem down the sides and across the bottom, then attach a length of lace at the bottom edge.

2 Turn over 1 cm (³⁄₈ in) at the top edge of the skirt. Sew two rows of gathering along the top edge. Pull up the gathering so the waist is 11.5 cm (4½ in). Stitch the skirt onto the doll, sewing a length of ungathered lace along the waist at the same time.

3 Stitch lace around the sleeve ends to make a cuff and across the neck to make a collar.

## To complete Sister 1

1 Cut twenty to twenty-four 1 cm x 6 cm (³⁄₈ in x 2³⁄₈ in) strips of the hair fabric. Stitch these flat around the head. Stitch twelve of the small buttons onto the head to cover the hair ends.

2 Stitch the hands together, then stitch them to the bodice in a praying position.

## To complete Sister 2

1 Cut off approximately 1 m (1¹⁄₈ yd) of Perle Cotton for the boot laces. Twist the remainder of the hank so that it covers the top of the doll's head and stitch it into position with a matching thread. Cut a 4 cm x 40 cm (1½ in x 15³⁄₄ in) strip of the second border fabric and tie it into a bow. Sew the bow into place.

2 Stitch the hands together holding the basket.

## Finishing

1 Cut out small pieces of fabric with the pinking shears. Write on them with the Pigma pens or the marker pens. Stitch the tags onto the top of the dolls' legs.

2 Cut the backing fabric and the Pellon or Rayfelt a little larger than the quilt top. Assemble the quilt sandwich, then quilt the wallhanging in a design that pleases you. Ours has been quilted in sunflowers, crows and birdhouses – mirroring the design on the fabrics.

3 Cut four 5.5 cm (2¹⁄₄ in) wide strips. Fold them over double with the wrong sides together. Stitch the binding to the right sides of the sides of the wallhanging with the raw edges even. Turn the binding to the back of the wallhanging and slipstitch it into place. Bind the top and the bottom in the same way.

4 Cut the socks from the piece of old sock or sweater and stitch them around the legs.

5 Using the Perle Cotton, make boot laces for Sister 1. Stitch the two buttons or beads onto the shoes of Sister 2 and two remaining small buttons on her dress bodice.

6 Stitch a casing to the back of the quilt and hang your quilt so the Sisters can watch over you.

# My Baskets

MADE BY FAY KING

*The baskets in this little quilt can hold all that you love, including all your favourite pastimes.*

**Finished size:** 130 cm (51 in) square

## Materials

- 1.4 m (1½ yd) of pink fabric for the background
- 75 cm (30 in) of cream and aqua fabric for the background
- 75 cm (30 in) of floral fabric
- 1.2 m (1⅓ yd) of blue fabric for the border
- small pieces of a large variety of cotton prints in lights and darks for the cotton reels
- 40 cm (16 in) of fabric for the binding
- 2.1 m (2¼ yd) of fabric for the backing
- small black beads for the flower centres
- embroidery thread for the bobbins
- silk ribbon, embroidery threads, scraps of lace and fabric and charms, as required, for the basket contents
- gum turpentine
- photograph
- paper towel
- spoon
- cotton wadding
- quilting thread
- Piecemakers betweens needles, size 9

## Construction

See the Templates on pages 32 and 33.

**Note:** The quilt is constructed in units. Make the four basket blocks first, then complete the appliqué for each basket, before joining the four basket blocks to complete the centre of the quilt.

### Cotton reel block (7.5 cm/3 in) square

1 Cut the following pieces:
one **A** from the cotton reel fabric
two **B** from the background fabric
two **B** from the cotton reel fabric
twenty-eight **C** from the floral fabric.

2 With the right sides together, make the cotton reel by joining one **A** and two **B**. Do not stitch right across, but begin and end 6 mm (¼ in) from the edges (Fig. 1).

3 Join in the two background **B** pieces (Fig. 2). Stitch them onto the centre square first, beginning and ending 6 mm (¼ in) from the edge. Stitch the diagonal seams. Make eighty-four blocks.

4 Assemble the corners of the quilt with twenty-one cotton reel blocks and seven **C** pieces in each corner (Fig. 3).

### Basket block

1 Cut the following pieces:
six **D** from the background fabric
twelve **D** from the basket fabric
one **E** from the background fabric
one **F** and one **Fr** from the background fabric.

2 Join each background **D** to a basket fabric **D** to form a square. Make six squares.

3 Make one each of unit **a**, unit **b** and unit **c**, using the additional six **D** in the basket fabric (Fig. 4).

4 Make two d units using **F**, **Fr** and two **D** from the basket fabric (Fig. 5).

5 Assemble the half block, adding the corner triangle **E** (Fig. 6).

6 From the background fabric, cut one triangle as shown in figure 7. Press under a 6 mm (¼ in) seam allowance on the long edge.

7 Make a cardboard template of the handle. Cut a 4 cm (1½ in) wide bias strip from the basket fabric. Baste the strip over the handle template allowing 6 mm (¼ in) to extend beyond each end of the template. Press well with a hot iron to crease the edges. Remove the basting and the handle template. Appliqué the handle to the large triangle, centring it carefully.

8 Join the two halves of the basket block. Make four basket blocks in the same way.

**Note:** If you have items to appliqué into the basket, appliqué these before completing step 8.

## Embroidery basket

### For the bobbins

1 Cut two thread bobbins from white scraps. Appliqué them in place, then stitch the embroidery thread on to give the appearance of a full bobbin.

2 Cut a 4 cm (1½ in) square from an embroidered lace for the pillow. Stitch 6 mm (¼ in) edging around the square and appliqué the pillow into position.

### For the family photo

1 Photocopy a small favourite photograph. Lay fabric on a piece of paper towel. Lay the photocopy face down on the fabric. Dampen the back of the photocopy with gum turpentine, then rub the back of the photocopy with the back of a spoon really hard until the photo is transferred.

2 Cut a piece of pink fabric for the mat. Cut out the centre oval to accommodate the photograph. Clip around the edges of the oval, then turn under the raw edge. Appliqué the framing mat over the photograph.

3 Appliqué a 6 mm (¼ in) picture frame, then appliqué the whole picture into the basket.

### For the crazy patchwork heart

1 Prepare a 10 cm (4 in) square of crazy patchwork. Cut a cardboard template, using the heart pattern provided. Cut the crazy patchwork to the heart shape with a generous seam allowance. Baste it onto the template. Press well, then remove the basting and the template.

2 Appliqué the heart into the basket. Trim it with a silk ribbon bow and brass charm or buttons.

## Picnic basket

### For the tablecloth

1 Cut a 10 cm (4 in) square of fabric on the diagonal. Stitch a 6 mm (¼ in) seam on the two short sides of one piece. Baste it into position on the basket base before joining the handle section.

2 The cup and saucer, plate, fruit and vegetables have been cut from fabrics, leaving a 6 mm (¼ in) seam allowance around each piece. Baste them into position, then appliqué by flipping the fabric under with the needle as you go.

## Flower basket

1 Using the patterns provided, cut the following pieces: two leaves (a) and two leaves (b).
For each pansy, cut one purple using template 1, one yellow using template 2 and one mauve using template 3. Cut nine daisy petals and one daisy centre.

2 For the bluebells, cut four 4 cm x 5 cm (1½ in x 2 in) rectangles of fabric. Fold them in half, with the right sides together so they are 2.5 cm x 4 cm (1 in x 1½ in). Stitch the longer sides together, then gather one end with a small running stitch. Turn the piece to the right side and fold

up a small hem at the base. Gather the base with small stitches. Appliqué the four bluebells onto the basket, then embroider a stem.

3 For the small flowers, cut three 4 cm (1½ in) diameter circles of fabric. Turn a tiny hem to the wrong side, then run a gathering stitch around the edge. Pull up the gathering really tightly. Secure the thread. Stitch a loop of thread over the edge of the pompom into the centre to pull the petal indentations into the flower. Make five petals. Stitch some beads into the centre. Appliqué the small flowers into place.

## Patchwork basket

1 Cut nine triangles from different fabrics, using the pyramid template and adding seam allowances. Piece a small pyramid with five triangles across the base (Fig. 8). Fold under the seam allowances on the outer edges. Appliqué the pyramid into the basket.

2 For the heart quilt, cut four tiny hearts, using the template provided. Appliqué the hearts onto a 6 cm (2½ in) square of the background fabric. Add a 6 mm (¼ in) border. Appliqué the heart quilt into the basket.

3 For the log cabin quilt, cut a 3 cm (1¼ in) square for the centre. Cut 2 cm (¾ in) wide strips of fabric, half light and half dark. Sew them around the square in the log cabin design, keeping the lights to one side and the darks to the other (Fig. 9). Turn under the raw edges on the outside. Appliqué the quilt into the basket.

## Finishing

1 Join the four basket blocks to form the centre panel. Square up the panel so it is 62 cm (24½ in) square.

2 For the borders, cut the following:
four strips 4 cm (1½ in) wide for border 1
four strips 4 cm (1½ in) wide for border 2
four strips 2.5 cm (1 in) wide for border 3
four strips 4 cm (1½ in) wide for border 4
four strips 9 cm (3½ in) wide for border 5.

3 For the border around the centre, join the border strips in sets of three, matching the centres. Attach the borders and mitre the corners.

4 Add the corner cotton reel sections.

5 Add the outer borders as before, joining the strips and matching the centres.

6 Quilt with your own choice of patterns.

7 Cut the binding strips 5 cm (2 in) wide. Join strips to achieve the required length. Fold the strips over double with the wrong sides together. With all the raw edges matching, sew the binding to the right side of two opposite sides of the quilt. Turn the binding to the back of the quilt. Bind the remaining two edges in the same way. Slipstitch the binding to the back of the quilt.

8 Attach a hanging sleeve. Don't forget to sign and date your quilt.

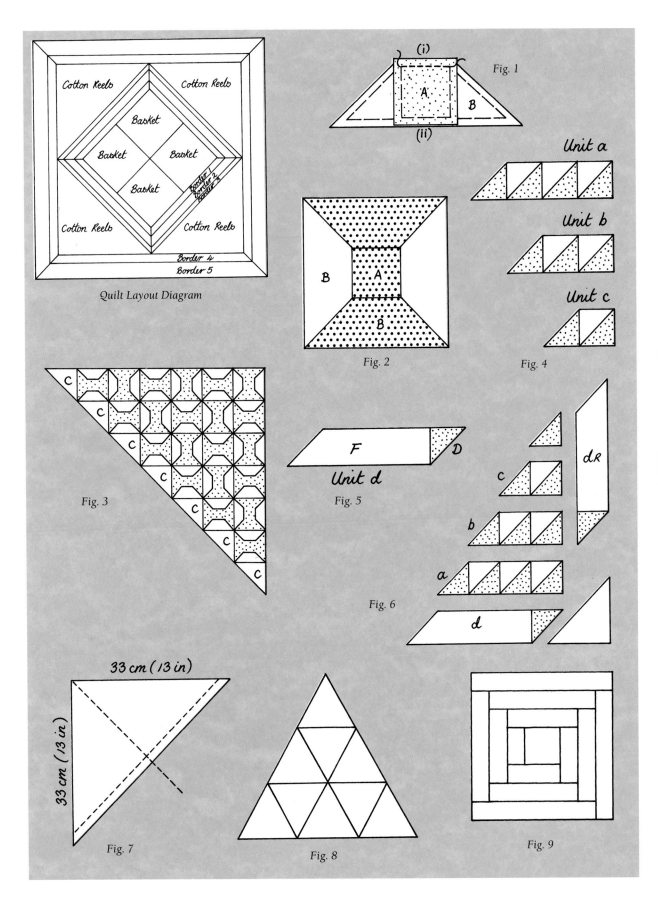

Cotton Reels    Cotton Reels

Basket

Basket    Basket

Basket

Border 1
Border 2
Border 3

Cotton Reels    Cotton Reels

Border 4
Border 5

Quilt Layout Diagram

Fig. 1

A    B

(i)
(ii)

Unit a

Unit b

Unit c

Fig. 2

B    A    B

Fig. 4

Fig. 3

Unit d
F    D
Fig. 5

c

dR

b

a

Fig. 6

d

33 cm (13 in)

33 cm (13 in)

Fig. 7

Fig. 8

Fig. 9

Leaf
Cut 2

Leaf
Cut 2

F

Basket Handle Template

Pansy 2
Yellow

Pansy 1
Purple

Pansy 3
Mauve

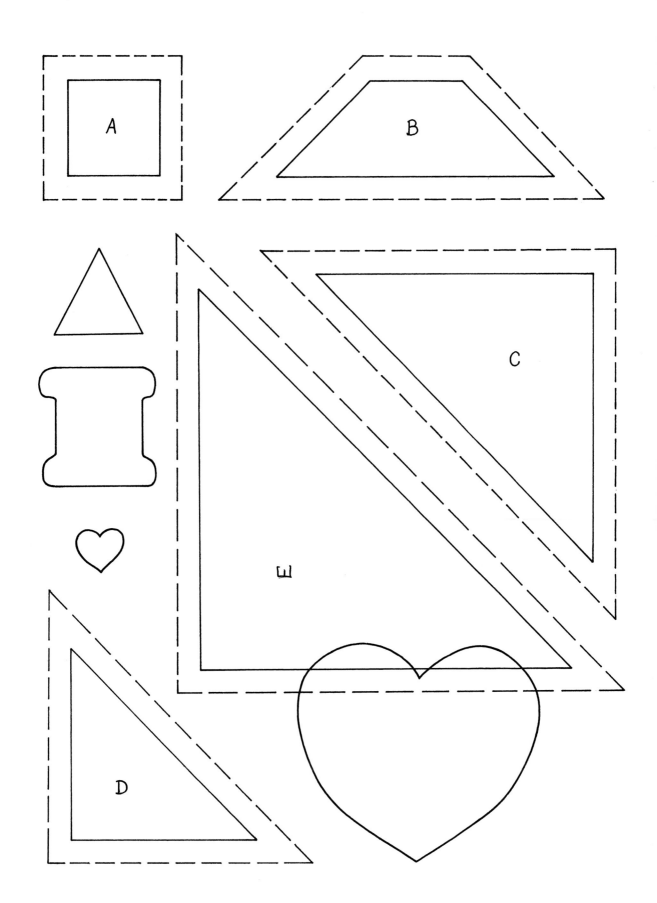

A

B

C

D

E

# Posies and Pansies

MADE BY PIECEMAKERS COUNTRY STORE, CALIFORNIA

*This beautiful appliqué block looks wonderful framed, made into a pillow or as the beginning of a fabulous appliqué quilt.*

**Finished block size:** 35.5 cm (14 in) square

## Materials

- 46 cm (18 in) of fabric for the background
- 11.5 cm (4½ in) of fabric for each pansy, or scraps of three fabrics
- 11.5 cm (4½ in) of fabric for flowers E and F
- scrap of fabric for the centre of F
- 11.5 cm (4½ in) of fabric for flowers G and H
- 11.5 cm (4½ in) each of three fabrics for the leaves
- embroidery floss for the stems
- fourteen buttons in a variety of sizes and colours
- 46 cm (18 in) each of wadding and fabric for the backing
- tracing paper
- black permanent fineline marker pen
- masking tape
- pencil
- cardboard or plastic for the templates

## Method

See the Patterns and Placement Diagrams on the Pull Out Pattern Sheet.

## Preparation

**1** Using the marker pen, trace the placement diagram from the pattern sheet. Cut a 36 cm (14½ in) square from the background fabric. Tape the tracing to a light box or a window in daylight and tape the fabric square over the top. Lightly trace the design onto the fabric, just inside the tracing lines so the pencil lines will be hidden under appliqué pieces.

**2** Make templates for all the pattern pieces.

**3** There are several methods for appliqué and the method you choose will affect the way you cut out and prepare the appliqué pieces:

If you intend to use 'needle-turn' appliqué, draw the pattern pieces onto the right side of the fabric with a 3 mm (⅛ in) seam allowance.

If you intend to use freezer paper or baste onto cardboard, draw the pattern pieces onto the right side of the fabric with a 6 mm (¼ in) seam allowance.

## Appliqué

Following the numbers on the placement diagram for the order, appliqué the pieces into place, using your chosen method, overlapping them as shown and attaching all the **D** leaves last of all. Don't attach the flower centres **G** and **H** at this stage.

## Embroidery

Embroider the stems in stem stitch, using two strands of embroidery floss.

## Finishing

Assemble the quilt sandwich. Sew the buttons onto the pansies, then sew on the flower centres **G** and **H**.

Have your picture framed as we have done or make it up into a pretty cushion.

# Silk Collage Memory Vest

DESIGNED AND STITCHED BY PAT FLYNN KYSER, ALABAMA

*This elegant vest features special photographs that have meaning to you, or to the intended recipient of your vest.*

## Materials

- ❧ photographs
- ❧ commercial vest pattern without darts
- ❧ sufficient homespun to cut two vest fronts
- ❧ sufficient solid-coloured taffeta to cut one vest back
- ❧ sufficient printed cotton fabric for lining
- ❧ freezer paper (the type sold in craft and patchwork shops)
- ❧ silk scraps or old neckties
- ❧ variety of hand- and/or machine-embroidery threads
- ❧ silk ribbon in a variety of colours and widths
- ❧ special tiny buttons, metal charms, scraps of lace, beads
- ❧ 1.22 m (1$^1$/$_3$ yd) of 2 cm ($^3$/$_4$ in) wide grosgrain ribbon
- ❧ 2.44 m (2$^2$/$_3$ yd) of 6 mm ($^1$/$_4$ in) wide grosgrain ribbon
- ❧ matching sewing threads

## Method

1 Cut out the front and back pieces from the homespun to use as a base. Set them aside for later use.

2 To transfer the photographs, cut a piece of homespun 21.5 cm x 28 cm (8$^1$/$_2$ in x 11 in) and a piece of freezer paper the same size. Iron the homespun to the waxed side of the freezer paper, then run this stiffened piece of fabric through a photocopier, copying the photos you have chosen onto it. Wait until the copy medium has had time to dry thoroughly, then cover the photos on the fabric with a pressing cloth and press to heat-set them. Cut them apart to use on your vest.

3 Using the pressed quilt method (described in steps 4 and 5) cover the vest fronts in oddly shaped scraps of silk. (If you use old ties, it is a good idea to take them apart and handwash the fabric, before using it.) Place the fabric photos into your collage, wherever they seem appropriate to the design. Work with both vest fronts, side by side, so that you make one side to complement the other, but do not mirror-image them.

4 Pin one silk scrap in place on one of the homespun vest fronts, right side up, then build around it with the other scraps, placing each new scrap right side down, sewing the joining seam, then flipping the new one right side up and pressing it in place. You can do this by hand or by machine.

5 When both vest fronts are covered, decorate all the seams with fancy stitching, either by hand or by machine. You can do a simple machine feather stitch, as Pat did, using a variety of silky-textured threads, or you can create an even more elaborate effect with hand-sewn decorative stitches and decorative threads.

6 Decorate around the photographs and other areas of the vest fronts with silk ribbon embroidery. Create nosegays and bouquets of flowers, adding additional embellishment in the form of bits of lace, tiny buttons, metal charms and beading.

7 Cut out the back of the vest. Break up the plain surface of the vest back by decorating it with several rows of machine-stitched grosgrain ribbon.

8 Cut out the vest linings. Follow the pattern instructions for the lining and for finishing the vest.

## Finishing

Select a central section of the back of the vest and create the illusion of crazy pieces by feather-stitching random shapes in a thread to match the taffeta. Stitch through both the taffeta and the lining, letting the feather stitches 'quilt' the vest. Wear and enjoy your beautiful memory vest, or give it away, as Pat did – to a special daughter-in-law!

# Morning at Nobby's Beach

STITCHED BY YAN PRING

*A delightful summer quilt in fresh blues and butter yellows. This simple two-block construction will take you all the way to a sunny beach where you might find stars in the sand.*

**Note:** For simplicity's sake, the instructions given here are for using the same fabric throughout the background. However, special effects can be achieved by changing the background in some sections (see photograph).

**Finished size:** approximately 127 cm x 157 cm (50 in x 62 in)

## Materials

- 1.3 m (1³⁄₈ yd) of fabric for the background
- 90 cm (36 in) in total of scraps of blue fabrics
- 15 cm (6 in) of yellow fabric for the stars
- 25 cm (10 in) of yellow fabric for the border
- 90 cm (36 in) of plaid fabric for the border
- 32 cm (12¹⁄₂ in) of fabric for the binding
- 127 cm x 157 cm (50 in x 62 in) of fabric for the backing
- 127 cm x 157 cm (50 in x 62 in) of wadding
- matching sewing threads
- Olfa cutter and self-healing mat
- scissors
- transparent ruler
- quilting thread
- Perle cotton, Yellow

## Construction

See the Templates on page 41.

**Note:** 6 mm (¹⁄₄ in) seam allowances are included in all measurements.

### For Block A, the Snowball block (Fig. 1)

1 Cut twenty-four 16.5 cm (6¹⁄₂ in) squares from the background fabric.

2 Cut ninety-six 6.5 cm (2¹⁄₂ in) squares from the blue scraps.

3 Place four blue squares in the corners of the background square, with the right sides together. Sew the diagonal seams as shown in figure 2.

4 Trim away the outer triangle, 6 mm (¹⁄₄ in) from the sewing line and fold the remaining triangle outwards to form the corner triangles. Press gently.

5 Make twenty-four blocks in the same way. Cut seven of these blocks in half (Fig. 3) and set them aside for the edge sections.

### For Block B, the Nine-patch block (Fig. 4)

1 Cut the background fabric and the blue fabric into 6.5 cm (2¹⁄₂ in) wide strips across the full width of the fabric. Join the strips into sets as shown in figure 5, then cut the sets into 6.5 cm (2¹⁄₂ in) sections.

2 Assemble the sections into nine-patch blocks. Make eighteen blocks.

*Quilt Layout Diagram*

**3** Make ten of the unit shown in figure 6, using sets from figure 5 and 3 cm x 16.5 cm (1¹/₄ in x 6¹/₂ in) side strips cut from the background fabric. Set them aside.

## Assembling

**1** Cut four 8 cm (3¹/₄ in) squares of background fabric for the outer corners. Piece all the blocks and the outer sections together, following the quilt layout diagram.

**2** Cut 4.5 cm (1³/₄ in) wide yellow strips for the inner border and 15 cm (6 in) wide strips of plaid fabric for the outer border. Sew on the borders, mitring the corners.

**3** Using the template provided, cut out four stars of each size, adding a seam allowance. Position the stars on the quilt. Using the Yellow Perle cotton, blanket stitch the stars into place, clipping into the corners and tucking under the raw edge as you sew.

## Quilting

**1** Layer the backing (face down), the wadding and the quilt top (face upwards). Baste or pin ready for quilting.

**2** Hand-quilt or machine-quilt diagonally through the blues. Outline quilt the borders and stars.

**3** When the quilting is completed, trim the backing and wadding even with the quilt top.

### For the binding

**1** Cut 6.5 cm (2¹/₂ in) wide strips across the width of the binding fabric. Join the strips to achieve the required length.

**2** Fold the strips over double, with the wrong sides together. Press.

**3** With all the raw edges even, sew the binding to the right side of two opposite sides of the quilt. Turn the folded edge of the binding over to the back of the quilt. Sew the binding strips to the remaining two sides of the quilt in the same manner. Slipstitch the binding into place on the back of the quilt.

Don't forget to sign and date your quilt.

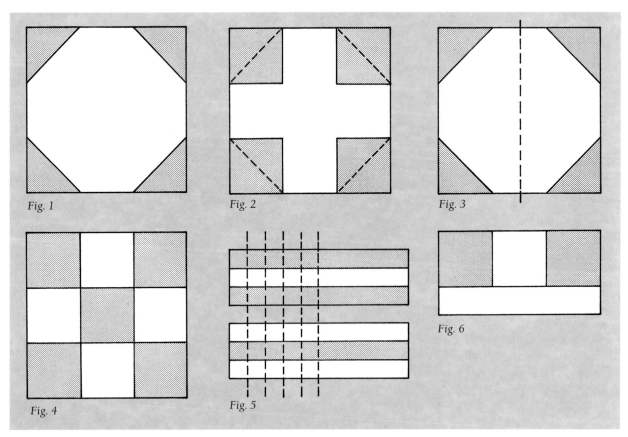

Fig. 1    Fig. 2    Fig. 3

Fig. 4    Fig. 5    Fig. 6

# Shoo Fly Star

MADE BY FAY KING

*This quilt is a wonderful way to use the treasures in your fabric stash.*

**Finished size:** 105 cm x 147 cm (41½ in x 58 in)

## Materials

- a variety of light, medium and dark fabrics in small, medium and large prints
- 1.5 m (60 in) of fabric for the border (you will only need 50 cm (20 in) if you are prepared to have joins)
- 1.5 m (1⅔ yd) of fabric for the backing
- 1.5 m (1⅔ yd) of wadding
- template plastic or cardboard
- marking pencil
- matching sewing thread
- quilting thread
- quilting needles

**Note:** This quilt has thirty-five 20 cm (8 in) blocks: eighteen Shoo Fly blocks and seventeen Variable Star blocks. For a larger quilt, simply add more blocks.

For the border fabric, a mixed colour such as this teal, rather than a pure colour such as blue, will usually work better for a scrap quilt.

## Method

See the Templates on pages 44-45.

## Cutting

1 Organise your fabrics into four piles: light, medium light, medium dark, and dark.

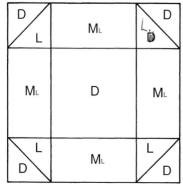

Fig. 1

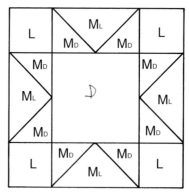

Fig. 2

| | |
|---|---|
| D | Dark |
| M_D | Medium - Darker |
| M_L | Medium - Lighter |
| L | Light |

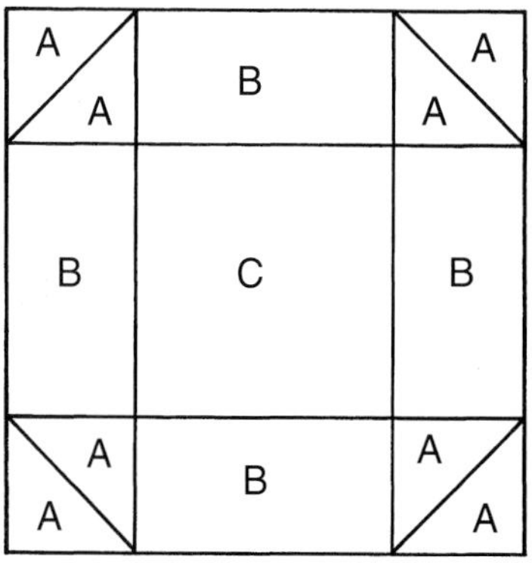

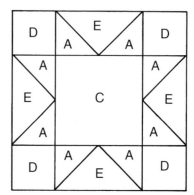

Fig. 3

Fig. 4

**2** Following figures 1, 2, 3 and 4 and using the templates provided, cut out the fabric for the blocks in the appropriate fabrics and quantities.

## Piecing

### For the Shoo Fly block

**1** Join a light and a dark triangle A four times to make four squares. Join a square to each end of two medium light rectangles B.

**2** Join a medium light rectangle B to opposite sides of a dark square C, then join the pieces made in step 1 to complete the block. Make eighteen blocks.

### For the Variable Star Block

**1** Join a medium dark triangle A to two sides of a medium light triangle E four times. Join a light square D to either end of two of these pieced rectangles.

**2** Join a pieced rectangle to two opposite sides of a dark square C, then join the pieces made in step 1 to the other two sides to complete the block. Make seventeen blocks.

### For the quilt top

**1** Join the blocks into rows, then join the rows, matching all the seams.

**2** Cut the borders 5 cm (2 in) wide by the length of the quilt top. Cut four 5 cm (2 in) squares and join these to the ends of the top and bottom borders. Sew on the side borders, then sew on the top and bottom borders.

## Quilting

**1** Assemble the quilt sandwich and baste ready for quilting.

**2** Scrap quilts were always made to be used, so the quilting was often quite basic. This quilt has been quilted with a Navy Blue thread in a lattice pattern, following the diagonal lines of the quilt.

**3** Trim the wadding to the size of the quilt top and the backing fabric 12 mm ($1/2$ in) larger than the quilt top. To finish the quilt edge, fold 6 mm ($1/4$ in) of the outer border in over the wadding. Fold the backing fabric in over the wadding. Slipstitch the quilt top and backing together.

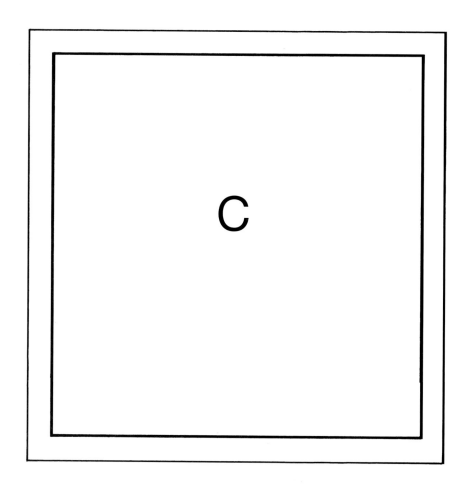

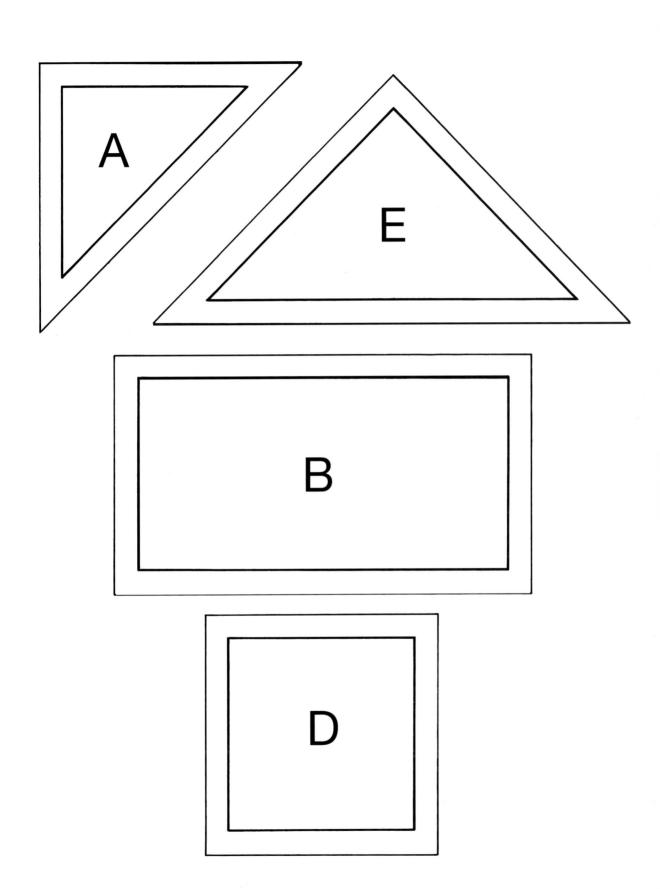

# A Passion for Purple

MADE BY YAN PRING

*This delightful colourwash heart is the perfect way to display those irresistible pansy prints.*

**Finished size:** 70 cm (27$\frac{1}{2}$ in) square

## Materials

- ✤ variety of pansy prints in large and small scale, dense and open designs
- ✤ 40 cm (16 in) of yellow/cream fabric for the background
- ✤ 20 cm (8 in) of lilac and black print fabric for the border
- ✤ 50 cm (20 in) of dark purple fabric for the outer frame
- ✤ 70 cm (28 in) of wadding
- ✤ sewing thread
- ✤ rotary cutter
- ✤ self-healing cutting mat
- ✤ quilter's ruler

## Method

**1** Using the rotary cutter and quilter's ruler, cut the pansy fabrics and the background fabric into 7 cm (2$\frac{3}{4}$ in) squares.

**2** Using the placement diagram and key on page 48, lay out all the squares to form the heart and background. Place open, leafy pansy prints around the outer edges to soften the outline of the heart.

**3** Following the construction diagram, sew the squares together into larger squares of four, then group these into squares of four, then join them into rows. Join the rows together to complete the quilt top. This method will be accurate and prevent distortion of the fabric. Press gently.

**4** Cut four dark purple float strips, 6 cm (2$\frac{1}{2}$ in) wide. Join these to the sides of the quilt.

**5** Have your hanging professionally framed for a perfect finish.

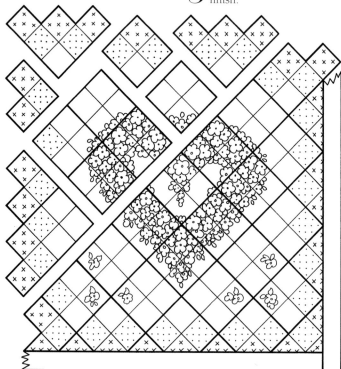

*Construction Diagram*

*Placement Diagram*

 *Pansy prints (dense)*

 *Pansy prints (open)*

 *Lilac and black print*

 *Dark purple plain*

 *Yellow/cream background*